Project Manager: Donna Salzburg
Cover Design: Joe Klucar

CONTENTS

ACROSS THE STARS
(LOVE THEME FROM *STAR WARS* ®: EPISODE II)

Music by
JOHN WILLIAMS

Across the Stars - 5 - 1

4

5

ARTHUR'S THEME
(Best That You Can Do)

Words and Music by
BURT BACHARACH, CAROLE BAYER SAGER,
CHRISTOPHER CROSS and PETER ALLEN

Once in your life, you'll find
Ar-thur, he does what he

Arthur's Theme - 4 - 1

AS TIME GOES BY

Words and Music by
HERMAN HUPFELD

As Time Goes By - 2 - 1

13

As Time Goes By - 2 - 2

BECAUSE YOU LOVED ME
(Theme from "Up Close & Personal")

Words and Music by
DIANE WARREN

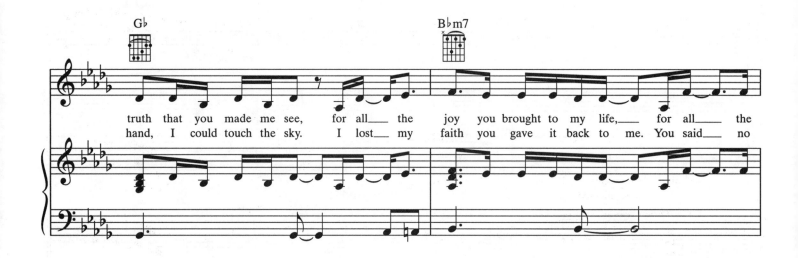

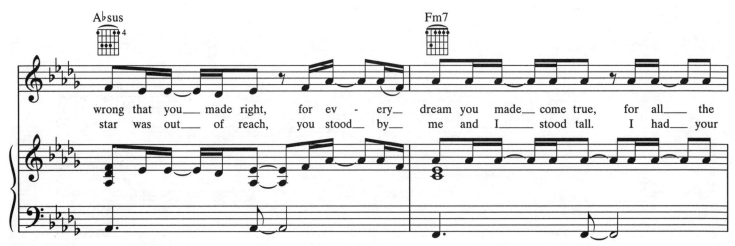

Because You Loved Me - 5 - 1

18

From the Twentieth Century Fox Motion Picture MOULIN ROUGE

COME WHAT MAY

Words and Music by
DAVID BAERWALD

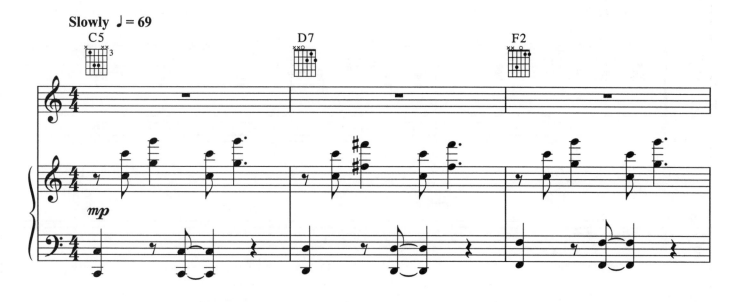

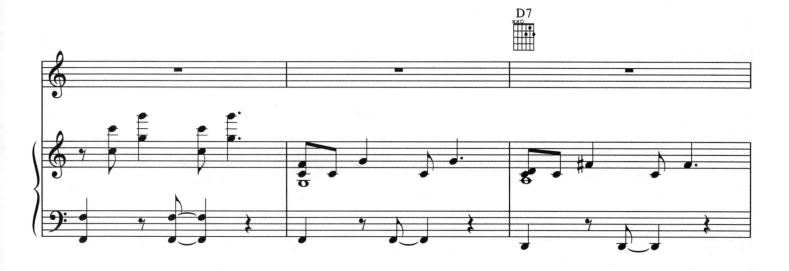

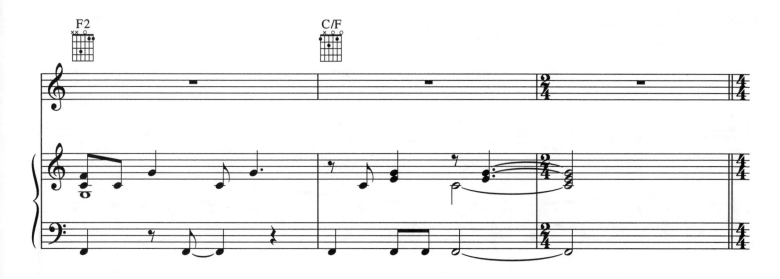

Come What May - 7 - 1

20

Verse 1:

(He:) 1. Nev - er knew I could feel like this, like I've___ nev - er seen___ the sky___

___ be - fore. Want to van - ish in - side your kiss.

Ev - 'ry day___ I love you more and___ more. Lis - ten to___ my heart.___ Can you

hear it sing, tell - ing me___ to give___ you ev - 'ry - thing.

Come What May - 7 - 2

22

Chorus:

THE ENTERTAINER
A Ragtime Two-Step

By
SCOTT JOPLIN

The Entertainer - 4 - 1

28

The Entertainer - 4 - 3

From Warner Bros. Pictures' HARRY POTTER AND THE CHAMBER OF SECRETS

FAWKES THE PHOENIX

Music by
JOHN WILLIAMS

Fawkes the Phoenix - 4 - 1

EYE OF THE TIGER
The Theme from ROCKY III

Words and Music by
FRANKIE SULLIVAN III and JIM PETERIK

Eye of the Tiger - 5 - 1

38

Eye of the Tiger - 5 - 5

A FOOL IN LOVE

Words and Music by
RANDY NEWMAN

A Fool in Love - 5 - 1

42

A Fool in Love - 5 - 4

GOLLUM'S SONG

as performed by Emiliana Torrini in the motion picture
"The Lord of the Rings: The Two Towers"

Words by FRAN WALSH
Music by HOWARD SHORE

Gollum's Song - 5 - 1

for all the lies you told us, the hurt, the blame.

And we will weep to be so a - lone. We are

lost. We can nev - er go____ home.____

So in the end I'll be what I will be.

Cm
D
No loy - al friend was ev - er there for me.
B/D♯
Bm/D
Now we say good - bye.
Cm
D
We say, you did - n't try.
Gm/D
Bm/D
These tears you cry have come too late.
mf
3

48

From Warner Bros. Pictures' HARRY POTTER AND THE SORCERER'S STONE

HEDWIG'S THEME

Music by
JOHN WILLIAMS

Hedwig's Theme - 5 - 1

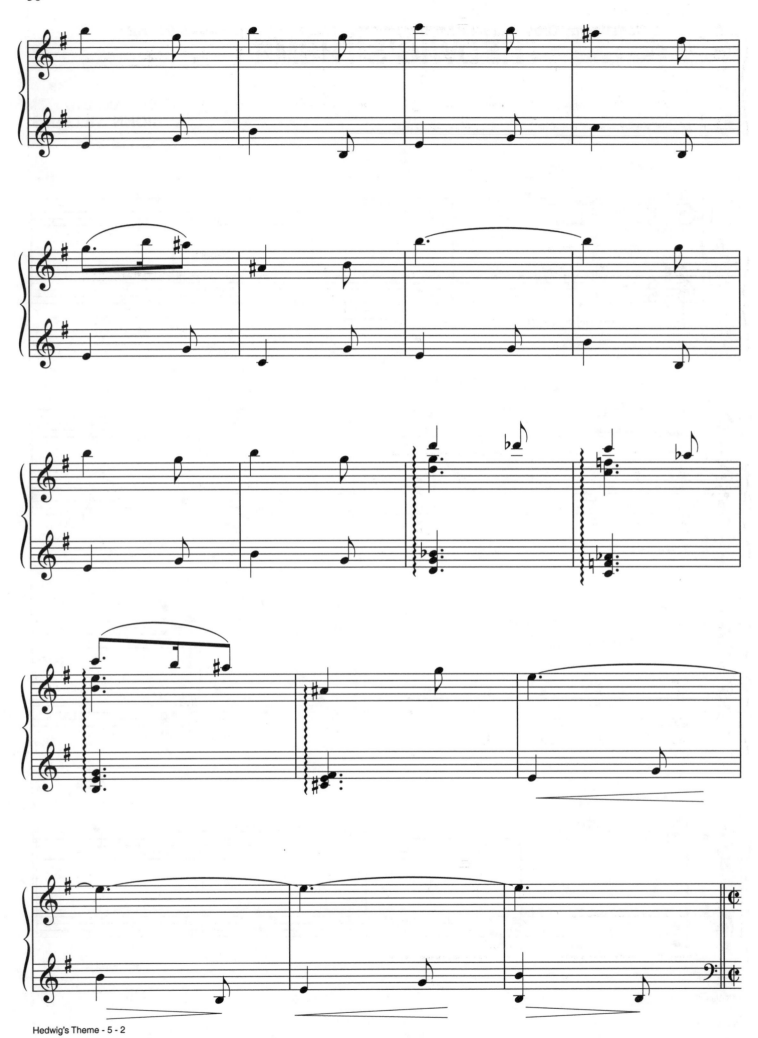

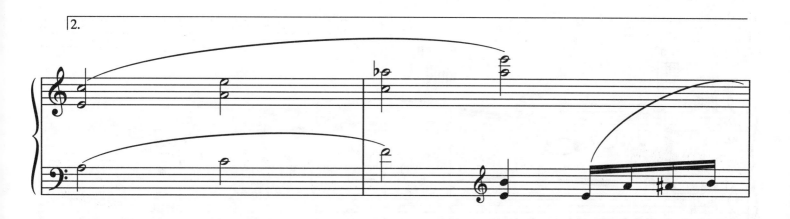

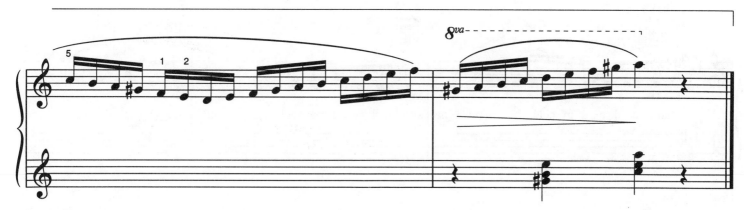

Hedwig's Theme - 5 - 5

From the Touchstone Motion Picture "CON AIR"

HOW DO I LIVE

Words and Music by
DIANE WARREN

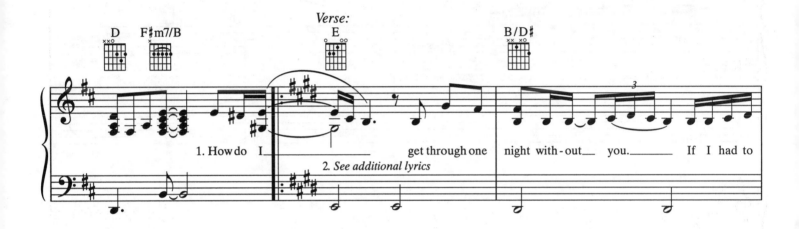

How Do I Live - 4 - 1

56

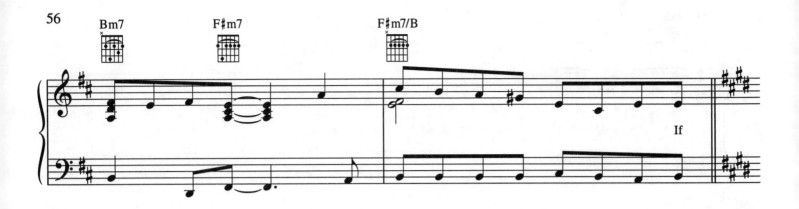

If

you ev - er leave,_____ ba - by, you would take a - way__ ev - 'ry - thing.__

Need you with me._____ Ba - by, 'coz you know that you're ev - 'ry - thing__

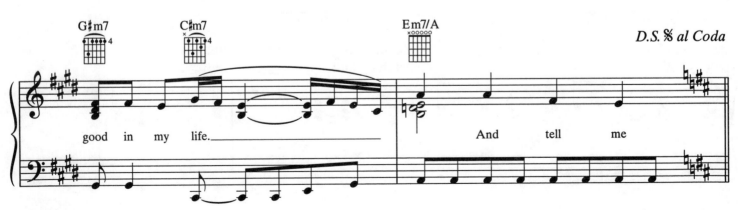

D.S. ℅ al Coda

good in my life._____ And tell me

⊕ Coda

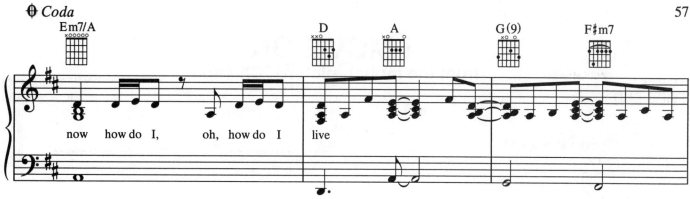

now   how do I,   oh, how do I   live

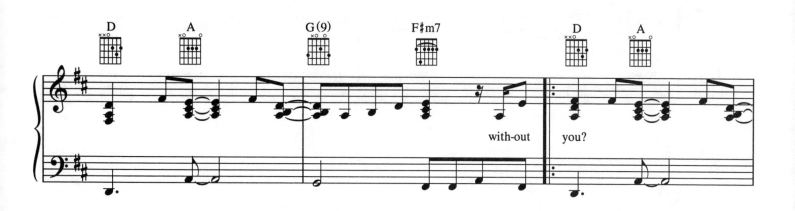

with-out   you?

Repeat ad lib. and fade
(vocal 1st time only)

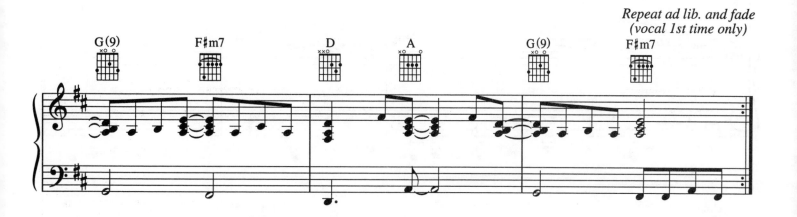

Verse 2:
Without you, there'd be no sun in my sky,
There would be no love in my life,
There'd be no world left for me.
And I, baby, I don't know what I would do,
I'd be lost if I lost you.
If you ever leave,
Baby, you would take away everything real in my life.
And tell me now...
(To Chorus:)

I MOVE ON
from the motion picture "Chicago"

Lyrics by
FRED EBB

Music by
JOHN KANDER

I Move On - 6 - 1

62

I Move On - 6 - 5

From Touchstone Pictures' ARMAGEDDON

I DON'T WANT TO MISS A THING

Words and Music by
DIANE WARREN

I Don't Want to Miss a Thing - 7 - 1

68

Chorus:

I Don't Want to Miss a Thing - 7 - 6

70

I Don't Want to Miss a Thing - 7 - 7

IN DREAMS
(featured in "The Breaking Of The Fellowship")

Words and Music by
FRAN WALSH and
HOWARD SHORE

In Dreams - 3 - 1

IT MIGHT BE YOU
(Theme From "Tootsie")

Words by
ALAN and MARILYN BERGMAN

Music by
DAVE GRUSIN

It Might Be You - 5 - 1

Chorus:

tell-ing me it might be _____ you. _____   1. 2. It's
3. It's

tell-ing me it might be _____ you. _____   2. All of my life; _____
tell-ing me it must be _____ you. _____

So man-y qui-et walks _____ to take. _____

So man-y dreams _____ to wake. _____ And we've so much love _____ to make _____

77

It Might Be You - 5 - 4

JAMES BOND THEME
(Bond vs. Oakenfold)

Music by MONTY NORMAN
Remix by PAUL OAKENFOLD

James Bond Theme - 5 - 1

80

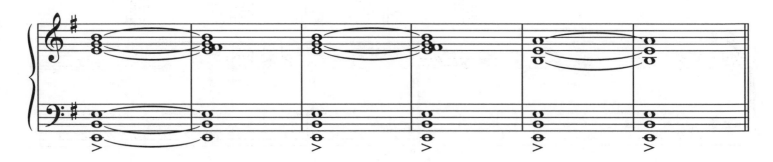

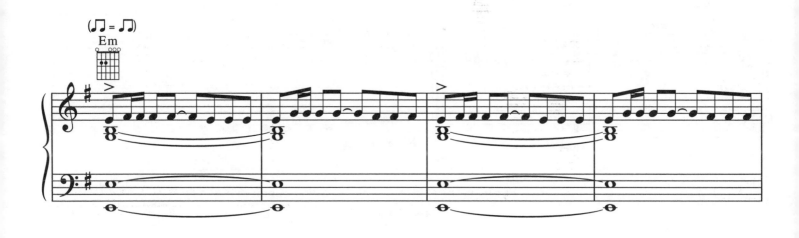

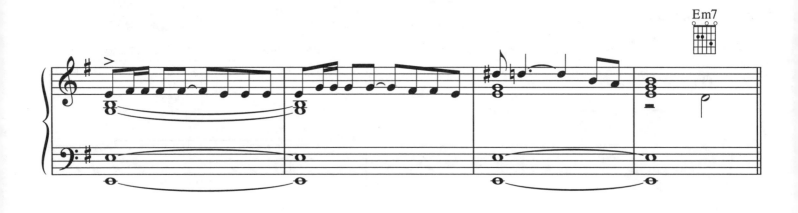

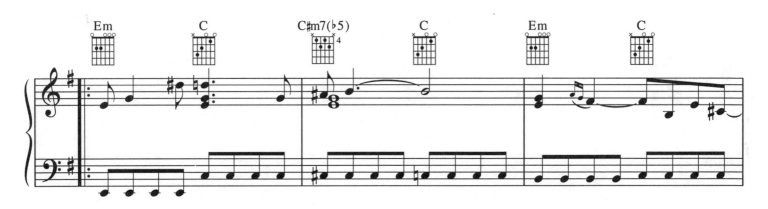

James Bond Theme - 5 - 4

OVER THE RAINBOW

Lyric by
E.Y. HARBURG

Music by
HAROLD ARLEN

Over the Rainbow - 4 - 1

METRO-GOLDWYN-MAYER presents DAVID LEAN'S FILM "DOCTOR ZHIVAGO"

SOMEWHERE, MY LOVE
(Lara's Theme From "Doctor Zhivago")

Lyric by
PAUL FRANCIS WEBSTER

Music by
MAURICE JARRE

Moderately

rit.

Verse: Ad lib.

Gm   D7   Cm

Where are the beau-ti-ful days?   Where are the sleigh-rides 'til dawn?

G7   G7-9   Cm   G7   Am7   D7

Where are the ten-der mo-ments of splen-dor? Where have they gone? Where have they gone?

Moderately with expression

G   Gdim   D7

Some-where, My Love   there will be songs to sing,

Somewhere, My Love - 3 - 1

Somewhere, My Love - 3 - 2

90

THE POWER OF LOVE

Words and Music by
JOHN COLLA, CHRIS HAYES and HUEY LEWIS

The pow-er of love___ is a cu-ri-ous thing;

The Power of Love - 7 - 1

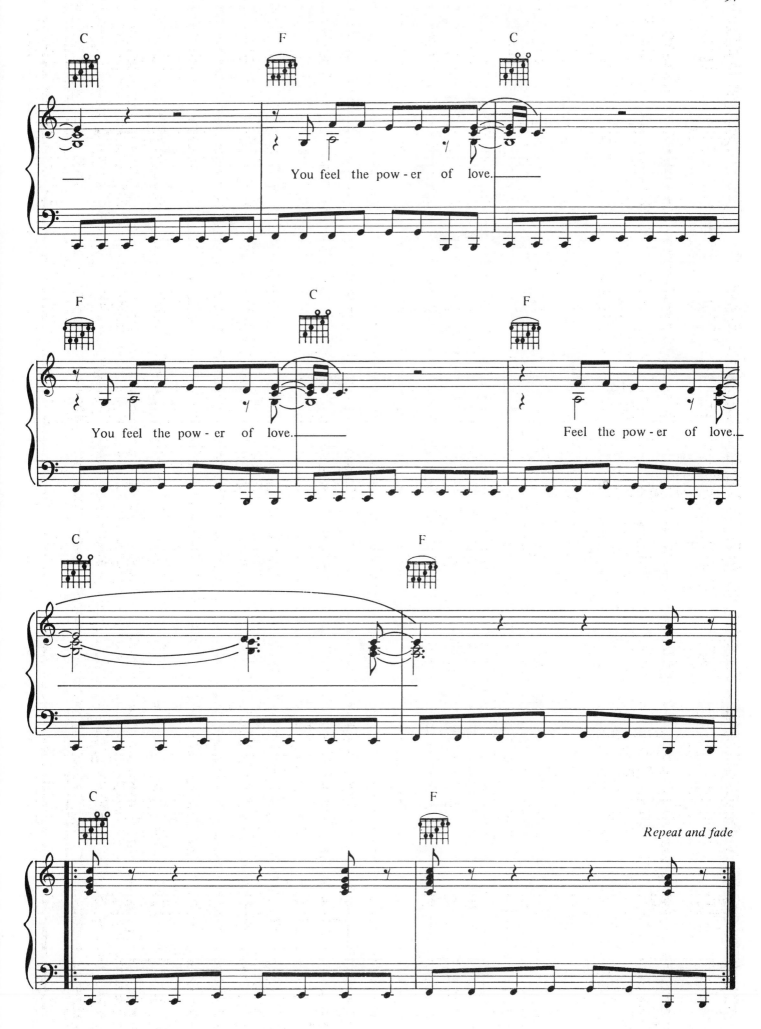

SOMEWHERE OUT THERE

Words and Music by
JAMES HORNER, BARRY MANN and CYNTHIA WEIL

Somewhere Out There - 5 - 1

through, then we'll be to - geth - er some-where out there, out

where dreams come true.

102

STAYIN' ALIVE

Words and Music by
BARRY GIBB, MAURICE GIBB
and ROBIN GIBB

Stayin' Alive - 5 - 1

THAT'S WHAT FRIENDS ARE FOR

Words and Music by
CAROLE BAYER SAGER and BURT BACHARACH

That's What Friends Are For - 3 - 1

109

That's What Friends Are For - 3 - 2

110

Ebadd9   Ebadd9/D   Db6(no 5th)   C7sus4   C7

For good - times, and bad_ times
in good - times, in bad_ times}   I'll be on_ your side for - ev - er

Cb6(no 5th)   Bb7sus4   Bb7sus4   To Coda

more.   That's what friends_ are for

Bb7sus4   D.S. al Coda

for.

Coda   Bb7sus4

for.

Repeat and fade
Vocal ad lib.

Ebmaj9   Ebmaj9/D   Ab(add Bb)/C   Gm7   Cm7   Fm7   Bb11

That's What Friends Are For - 3 - 3

From Touchstone Pictures' PEARL HARBOR

THERE YOU'LL BE

Words and Music by
DIANE WARREN

Slowly ♩ = 69

(with pedal)

1. When I

Verse:

think back on___ these times___ and the dreams we left___ be-hind,___ I'll be
showed me how___ it feels___ to feel the sky with-in___ my reach.___ And I

glad 'cuz I___ was blessed___ to get,___ to have you in my___ life.___ When I
al-ways will___ re-mem-ber all___ the strength you gave to___ me.___ Your love

There You'll Be - 5 - 1

THE WIND BENEATH MY WINGS

Words and Music by
LARRY HENLEY and JEFF SILBAR

The Wind Beneath My Wings - 7 - 1

glo - ry, while you___ were the

no - ticed, but I've___ got it

one with all___ the strength.

all here in___ my heart.

A beau-ti-ful face with-out___ a name___ of

I want you to know I know___ the truth,___

for so long,___ a beau-ti-ful smile to hide___ the

course I know___ it, I___ would be noth - ing with - out

120

The Wind Beneath My Wings - 7 - 5

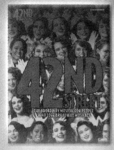